I0096563

Ocean Creatures & Painted Moments

ADULT COLORING BOOK WITH POETRY AND SELF-DISCOVERY

Aventuras De Viaje

Copyright SF Nonfiction Books © 2024

All Rights Reserved

No part of this document may be reproduced without written consent from the author.

www.SFNonfictionBooks.com

INTRODUCTION

Welcome to a realm where the ocean's heartbeat echoes, where the sublime grace of marine life merges with the magical spectrum of colors. This is more than a coloring book—it's a voyage, a sanctuary, and a homage to the myriad and spellbinding ocean creatures.

Each page draws you deeper into the heart of the ocean, where whales, dolphins, sea turtles, and countless others glide through the cerulean depths. These beings, emblems of power, elegance, and the wild essence of nature, await your touch of color to spring to life. Coloring these marvels offers not just an artistic odyssey but also a profound connection to the ocean's untamed allure.

In the hustle of daily life, pausing to breathe deeply is essential. Coloring affords a moment to decelerate, to immerse, and to renew our bond with the earth's natural wonders. It's an invitation to unleash a youthful sense of awe and illuminate it with a kaleidoscope of hues.

Embrace this artistic voyage, plunging into the oceanic expanse and the soothing practice of coloring. Here, you're not merely traversing an ecosystem; you're uncovering the delights of creativity and the serenity of mindfulness.

Discovering the Mosaic of Imagination

Dive deeper, and you'll find that this book has been meticulously crafted to enhance your personal journey:

- **Simple Activities:** Beyond just coloring, engage with activities designed to spark reflection and creativity. These gentle prompts will lead you to moments of introspection, serving as kindling for your inner fire.

- **Quotes:** Let the wisdom of personal development accompany you, illuminating your path as you add your own burst of color to the pages.

- **Positive Affirmations:** As you color, let these words of positivity uplift your spirit, molding your thoughts and inspiring a brighter perspective.

- **Poems and Haikus**: Delight in the poetic tales that complement the theme of this book, capturing life's varied rhythms and experiences. Each verse and every line serve as a muse for your artistic endeavors, enhancing your coloring journey with lyrical inspiration.

Embark on this coloring odyssey, immersing yourself in a world of diverse themes and the therapeutic embrace of art. Each page invites you on a unique journey, blending your creativity with the tranquility of coloring.

THANKS FOR YOUR PURCHASE

Get Your Next SF Nonfiction Book FREE!

Claim the book of your choice at:

www.SFNonfictionBooks.com/Free-Book

You will also be among the first to know of all the latest releases, discount offers, bonus content, and more.

Go to:

www.SFNonfictionBooks.com/Free-Book

Thanks again for your support.

Mirrored Moments:
Reflect on a moment today where you saw a part of yourself in someone else. What did it teach you about empathy or understanding?

_____

_____

"The ocean teaches us to flow with change, not against it."

I grow and evolve with each passing day, embracing the journey of self-discovery.

In the ocean's heart, mysteries unfold,
Depths unknown, stories untold.
Each creature a wonder, a sight to behold,
In the water's embrace, we find our
courage bold.

Acts of Kindness:
Describe a kind act you witnessed or did today.

_____

_____

"Find clarity in the chaos, like the calm beneath the waves."

I am in harmony with the rhythm of life, moving fluidly through each moment.

Sea's secret whispers,
Moonlit waves kiss sandy shores,
Night's serene chorus.

Challenge Overcome:
Recall a challenge you faced today.
How did you overcome it, and
what did you learn from the
experience?

_____

_____

"Harmony with oneself is like the ocean's balance - deep, vast, and serene."

I am connected to everything, a part of the vast web of life, from the ocean floor to the stars.

With every tide's rise and fall,
The ocean dances, mesmerizing all.
Its waves, a melody of call,
To the souls seeking to be
enthralled.

Dreams and Daydreams:
Think about a dream you had last
night or a daydream from today.
What could it be telling you about
your desires or fears?

_____

_____

"Embrace the currents of life as the sea embraces its waves."

I am the artist of my life; each day is a blank canvas to create something beautiful.

Deep sea's silent glow,
Creatures of light drift below,
Secrets they bestow.

Anchor of Stability:
What keeps you grounded and stable?

_____

_____

"Navigate your life with the same courage a sailor explores the sea."

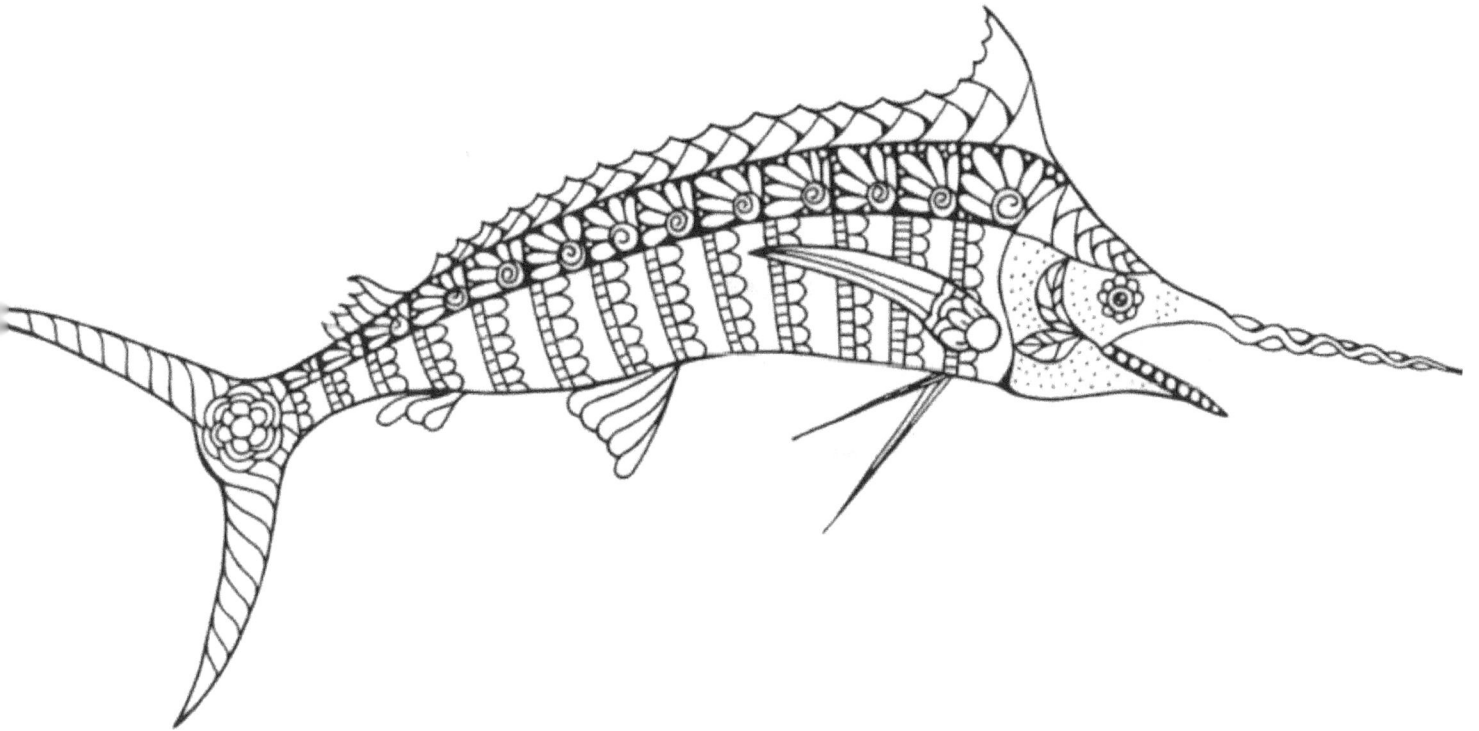

I am a beacon of light and hope, guiding like a lighthouse through the dark.

Beyond the shore,
where waves softly roar,
Lies a world to explore,
from the ocean floor.
Each tide, a door, to myths of yore,
In the sea's core, wonders galore.

Sail of Solitude:
How did you find peace or solace in solitude today?

_____

_____

"Be like water: adaptable, powerful, and persistent."

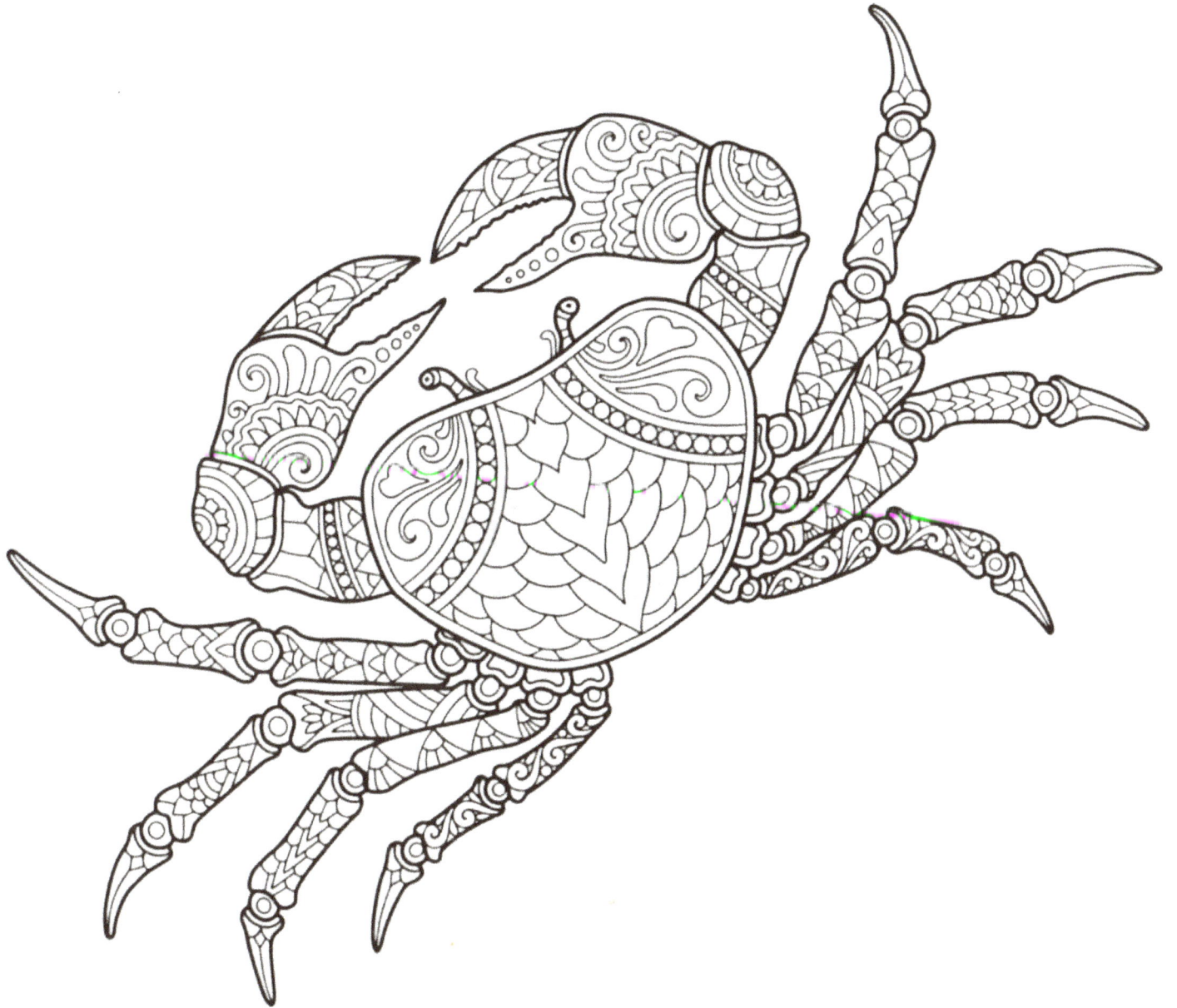

I embrace change with the grace of the tides, knowing it brings new beginnings.

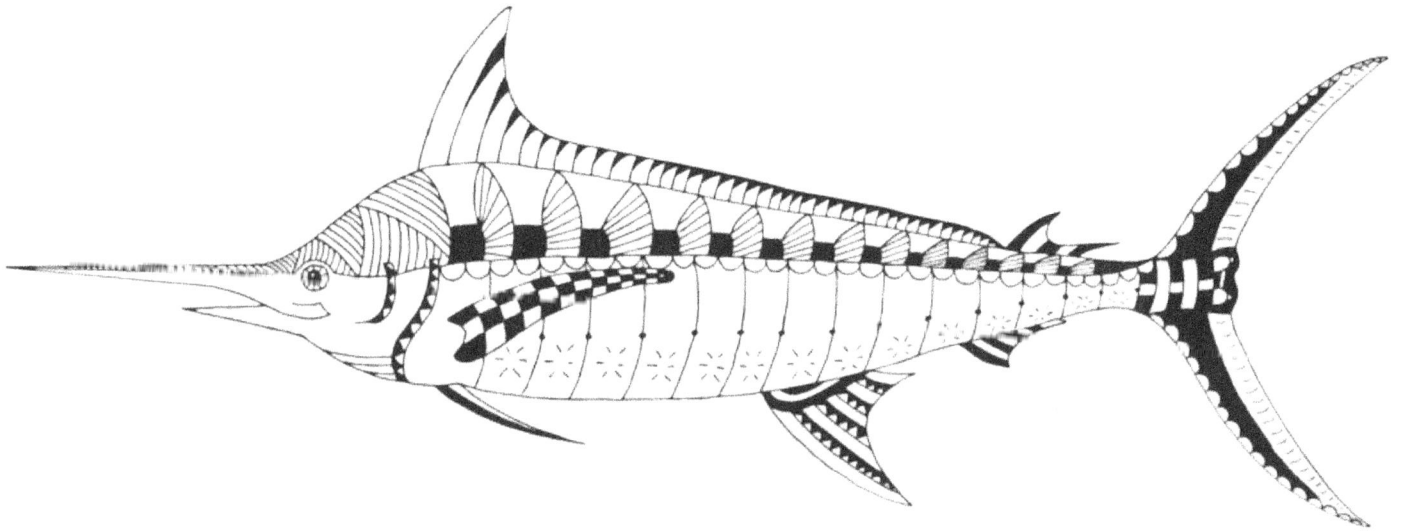

Starfish in the sand,
Guiding lost sailors to land,
Nature's helping hand.

Gratitude Tide:
For which moment today are you most grateful?

_____

_____

"In the ocean of life, resilience is our buoyancy."

I am adaptable, embracing life's ebbs and flows with ease and grace.

The moonlit sea whispers to me,
Tales of the deep, wild and free.
Its secrets, a spree, a key,
To understanding the ocean's plea.

Lesson from Nature:
Reflect on a lesson you learned
from nature today. How does it
apply to your life or perspective?

_____

_____

"Water is the driving force of all nature."

- *Leonardo da Vinci.*

I find clarity in introspection, diving deep into the ocean of my soul.

I find clarity in introspection, diving deep into the ocean of my soul.

Horizon of Hope:
What fills you with hope when you look ahead?

_____

_____

"Breathe in courage, exhale fear, just as the ocean embraces change with each tide."

I celebrate each moment,
treasuring life's fleeting beauty as
one treasures a rare seashell.

In the ocean's embrace, a symphony plays,
A melody of days, in the underwater maze.
Each wave sways, in the sun's rays,
Singing the ocean's praise, in myriad ways.

Sunrise/Sunset Gratitude:
Think of something you're grateful
for that began or ended today,
like the sunrise or sunset.

_____

_____

"Water can flow, or it can crash.
Be water, my friend."

- *Bruce Lee.*

I radiate kindness and compassion, echoing the nurturing nature of the seas.

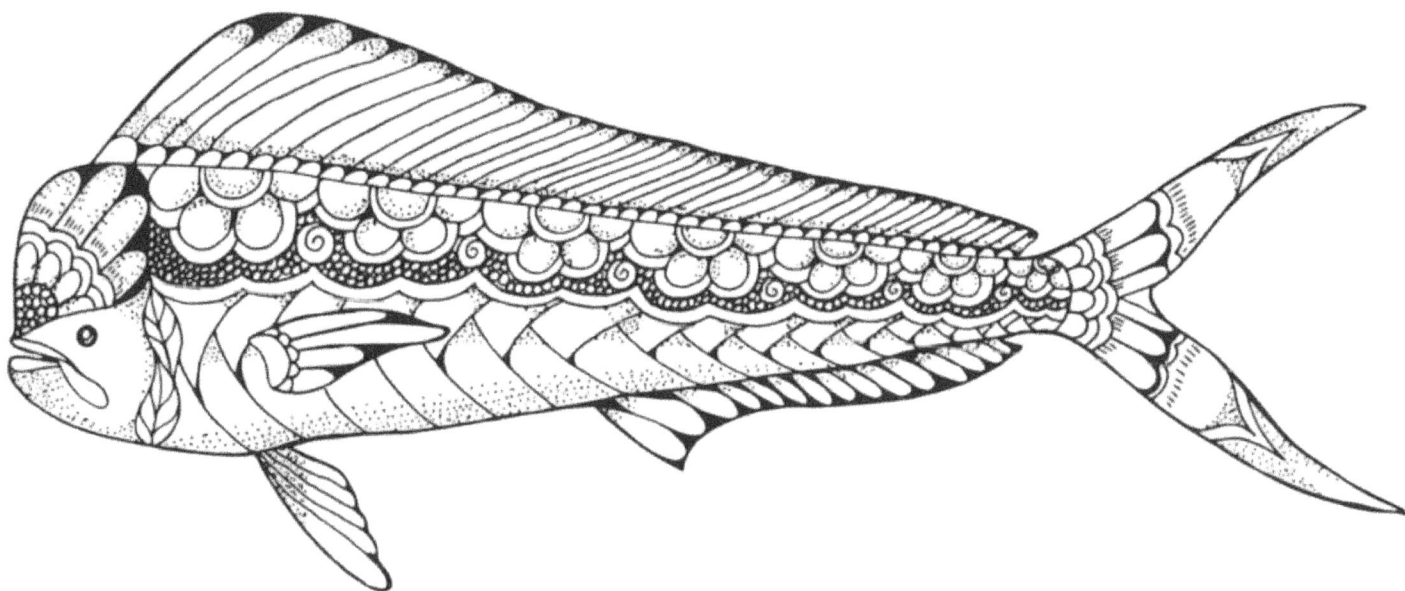

Waves whisper to shore,
Ocean's murmur, ancient lore,
Forevermore.

Compass of Curiosity:
What new thing did you feel curious about?

_____

_____

"Like the tides, our lives are in constant motion, ever changing, ever flowing."

I foster my inner peace, undisturbed by the chaos of the outside world.

In the ocean's hug,
Secrets deep, a cozy rug,
Heartstrings gently tug.

Silent Strength:
Consider a moment today when
silence spoke louder than words.
What did it communicate to you?

_____

_____

"Empty your mind, be formless, shapeless – like water."

- *Bruce Lee.*

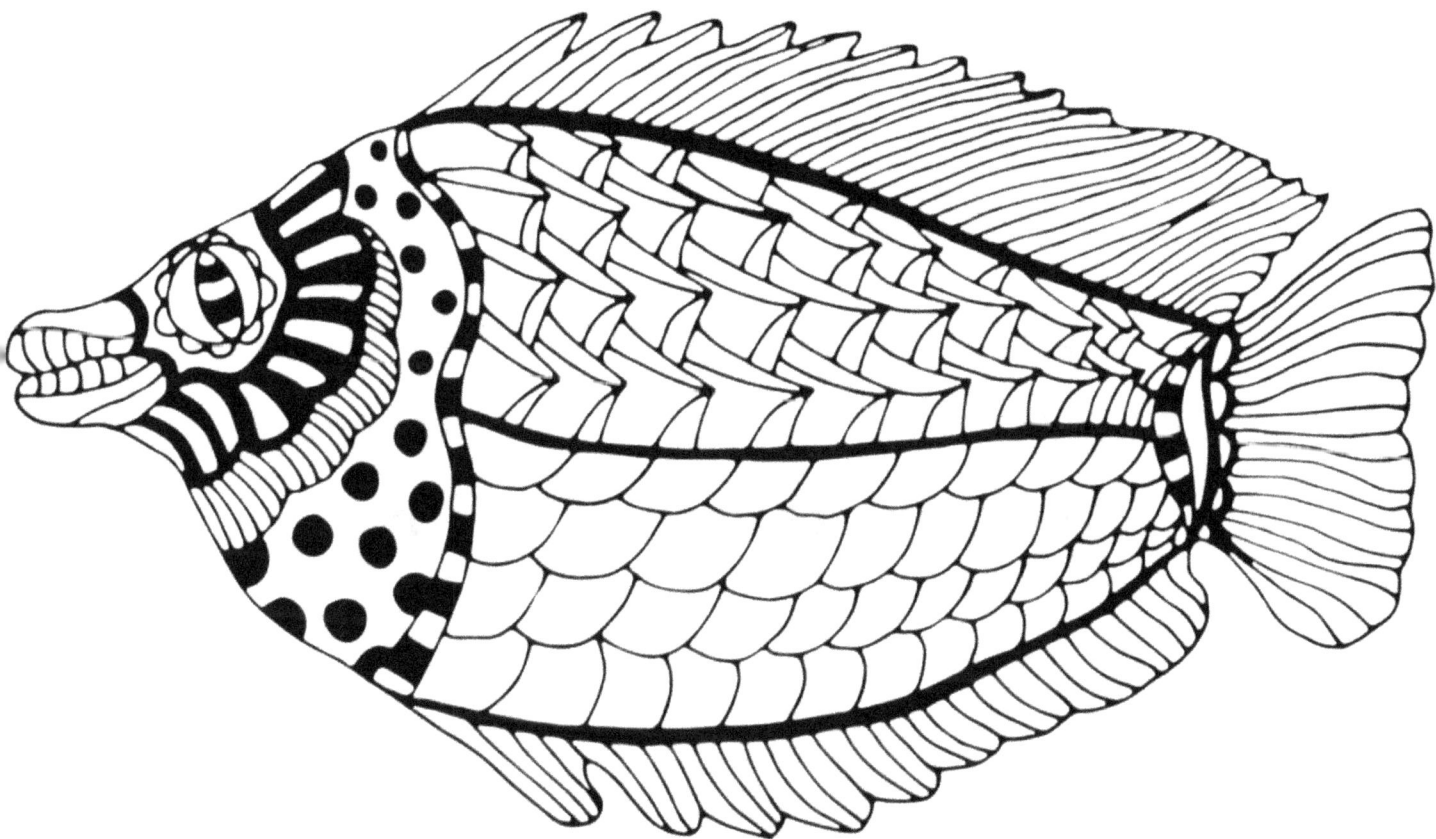

I embrace my journey with courage, exploring the unknown with excitement and joy.

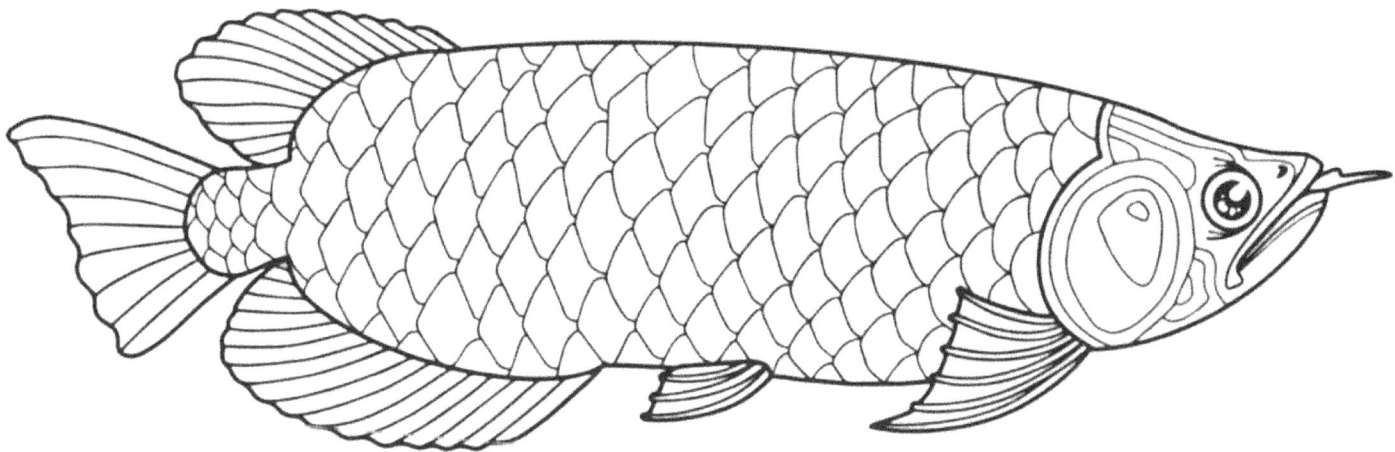

Where starfish dance, and corals beam,
Lies a world, serene, in a deep-sea
dream.
The water's gleam, a silvery stream,
Where seabed dreams, are not what they
seem.

Mindful Moment:
Recall a moment you were fully present today. What were you doing, and how did it make you feel?

_____

_____

"The calmness of the ocean mirrors the peace within us."

BEYOND THESE PAGES

A Deeper Dive into Art and Soul Awaits!

This book is but a chapter in a voyage where creativity meets depth.

Craving more? Explore the link below and weave deeper into the tapestry of art and emotion.

www.SFNonfictionBooks.com/Adult-Coloring-Books

A HEARTFELT THANK YOU

As the colors on these pages have come to life, so has our shared journey in this artistic realm. I am deeply grateful for your trust in choosing this book, and more so for allowing it to be a part of your self-care and personal journey.

Taking time for oneself is a gift—a silent promise of growth, introspection, and rejuvenation. By picking up the colors and filling these pages, you've not just created art but have also woven moments of peace, reflection, and creativity into your life.

Thank you for making space for yourself, for embracing the wonders within these pages, and for dancing to the rhythm of the lines and hues within this book. Your journey here is a testament to the beauty of dedicating time to one's soul and spirit.

If you enjoyed this journey and wish to explore more, know that there are other themes awaiting your artistic touch. Dive into new worlds and let your imagination flow.

From the deepest corner of my heart, thank you for bringing this book to life. Until our next artistic adventure together, cherish the colors of your journey and continue to shine.

Warmly,

Aventuras De Viaje

ABOUT THE AUTHOR

Aventuras has three passions: travel, writing, and learning new skills.

Combining these three things, Miss Viaje spends her time exploring the world and learning about anything and everything that interests her, from yoga, to music, to science, and more.

Aventuras takes what she discovers and shares it through her books.

www.SFNonfictionBooks.com

www.ingramcontent.com/pod-product-compliance
Lightning Source LLC
Chambersburg PA
CBHW080422030426
42335CB00020B/2548